W9-BNP-368

Mosaics Inside and Out

ROCKPORT

GLOUCESTER MASSACHUSETTS

ROCKPORT PUBLISHERS

Mosaics Inside and Out

Patterns and Inspiration
for 17 Mosaic Projects

Doreen Mastandrea

text by Livia McRee

First published in the United States of America by
Rockport Publishers, Inc.
33 Commercial Street
Gloucester, Massachusetts 01930-5089
Telephone: (978) 282-9590
Facsimile: (978) 283-2742
www.rockpub.com

ISBN 1-56496-742-5

10 9 8 7 6 5 4 3 2 1

Design: Dardani Gasc Design
Cover Image: Picture Press: Schöner Wohnen. Photo: R.C. Stradtmann

Printed in China.

ACKNOWLEDGMENTS

I would like to acknowledge the artists who contributed to this book: Twyla Arthur, Linda Benswanger, Sara Curtis, George Fishman, Melissa Glen, Stephanie Jurs and Robert Stout, Sonia King, Deb Mandile, Andrew Martin, Robin Millman, Aimee Southworth, Susan Strouse, and Bruce Winn.

I also want to thank the behind-the-scenes fabricators: Rosemary Broton Boyle, Dawn Dimadona, Michelle Fino, Carole Martin, Michael Roseberry, Jennifer West, and Michael Wilson.

Regina Grenier gets a special thanks for working so hard on this project, lending her insight and experience to the look of the book. Thanks, too, to Silke Braun, art director; to Shawna Mullen and Mary Ann Hall, my editors at Rockport Publishers; to illustrator Mary Newell DePalma; and to Bobbie Bush of Bobbie Bush Photography, for fun photo madness, great tunes, and chocolate.

I extend a special acknowledgment to the writer Livia McRee. Thanks again for all your hard work.

This book is dedicated to my family, to my friends, and to Harry and Susan.

Contents

Introduction

Mosaic is the process of laying pieces of glass, ceramic, stone – and just about anything else – into a bed of adhesive, such as cement. Mosaics are created piece by piece, similar to the way the dots of color make up a printed picture. This affords a mosaicist tremendous control; you can achieve great detail using fairly simple techniques. Tesserae (singular, tessera) is the collective name for the tiles used to create a mosaic picture.

People have been making mosaics, in one form or another, all over the world for thousands of years. Mosaic art as we know it began with the ancient Greeks. The Greeks paved and decorated floors with mosaics consisting of worn pebbles arranged in simple patterns. The Romans absorbed this skill, transforming it in their own way, and spread the art of mosaic across Europe.

When glass was brought into the picture, more detailed and complex mosaics were possible because of the smaller size of the tiles and the variety of color. Gorgeous works of mosaic art, both ancient and modern, adorn public and private domains. It is well worth the effort to investigate this branch of art history for inspiration when designing a mosaic!

A finished mosaic often looks intimidating to create, because it involves placing so many tiles. But even a beginner can make a stunning mosaic with a little practice and patience. The techniques involved are really quite simple, and there are only a few tools and materials needed to begin: a pair of nippers to shape the tiles, cement or grout, a surface to mosaic, and an assortment of broken ceramics, store-bought tiles, or found objects.

Mosaics are equally at home indoors and out. The projects in this book are intended to guide the beginner, and to inspire the more experienced mosaicist, to create beautiful works of art that enhance everyday life. The numerous tips, tricks, and professional advice throughout *Mosaics Inside and Out* will ensure that the effort put into a project results in a durable, lasting piece.

Now, let's get started!

Essential Tools & Materials

1 HAMMER

Use a hammer for breaking large ceramic pieces into smaller ones. First, wrap the pieces to be smashed in a towel to prevent shards from flying, and always wear safety goggles.

2 GLASS CUTTER

Use a simple glass cutter like this one to create straight edges on stained glass, vitreous glass, and mirror tiles. Use a ruler and a grease pencil to measure and mark the glass for cutting. Then, use firm, even pressure to score the glass with the cutter along the mark. Next, lightly tap the glass along the scoring with the ball end of the cutter, then gently snap the glass into two pieces.

3 CRAFT KNIFE

A craft knife is the best tool for scraping off dried adhesive that has accidentally spilled onto the tops of tiles. A craft knife is also useful for cleaning away any extra adhesive that is clogging up the crevices between tiles before grouting a project.

4 PAINT SCRAPER

A paint scraper is just one of many tools that can be used as an adhesive spreader. A palette knife or craft stick also works well. Always clean the scraper with water immediately after using it, because it is difficult to remove adhesive after it has dried.

5 BLACK UTILITY KNIFE

If a larger area needs to be scraped clean of dried adhesive, use a standard utility knife rather than the smaller blade of a craft knife.

6 HEAVY-DUTY UTILITY KNIFE

A heavy-duty utility knife is the best tool for cutting cement board, which is used to make the entryway on page 46 and the sign on page 45. First, deeply score both sides of the board with the knife, then snap the excess off. To do this, simply align the score mark with the edge of a table, then apply pressure to the pieces that extend past the table's edge.

7 NIPPER WITH RED HANDLE

This smaller-bladed nipper gives more control, which is essential when cutting irregularly shaped tiles.

8 SCORER AND PLIER

This combination scorer and plier has a wheel attached to the front that is used to score the piece to be cut. Grasp the tile with the tool and align the scoring with the guide mark. Press firmly, and the tile will break along the scoring. Use this tool for cutting pieces when straight lines are called for.

9 NIPPER WITH YELLOW HANDLE

A tile nipper is the basic tool used for cutting ceramic, marble, and glass pieces into basic shapes. A nipper is perfect for cutting straight-edged tiles, such as triangles, or for halving or quartering square tiles. Nippers are also used to custom-cut tiles for hard-to-fit areas.

10 CHIPPER NIPPER

This chipper nipper acts as a mosaic scissors. Use it to refine the shape of tiles and to make curved pieces such as circles or semicircles.

SAFETY & CLEAN-UP EQUIPMENT

1 BUCKET
Buckets of various sizes are perfect for mixing and transporting cement or grout. Set aside several for mosaic use only.

2 YELLOW SPONGE
Large sponges are crucial for wiping away grout effectively, which prevents filmy build-up. Wipe away grout continually as you work to prevent it from drying on tile surfaces.

3 GREEN SPONGES
Ordinary kitchen scrubbing pads can be used to sand grout to a perfect finish. Use the pads dry so as not to soften or smear the grout, and always wear a filter mask when sanding.

4 GOGGLES
Safety goggles are important to wear when cutting glass or ceramics to protect the eyes from the inevitable shards.

5 WHITE MASK
Filter masks are a necessary precaution because of the fine particles generated during mosaic work, especially when sanding grout.

6 TOWEL
A lint-free cloth is the best thing to use for buffing glass tiles after grouting. Buffing rids the surface of any residual grout film.

7 LATEX GLOVES
Latex gloves help prevent cuts and scrapes when working with sharp and jagged materials like glass and ceramic shards. They allow more control than kitchen gloves, which is helpful when applying grout by hand rather than with a tool.

8 DUSTPAN, BROOM
A small dustpan and broom are essential for keeping a workplace tidy and for whisking away broken bits of tile. If an area is particularly dusty, use a damp sponge to clean up rather than sweeping.

9 RUBBER GLOVES
Durable kitchen gloves protect hands when mixing or applying grout and cement. Also wear them when using a large sponge and water to wipe off excess grout from the tops of tiles.

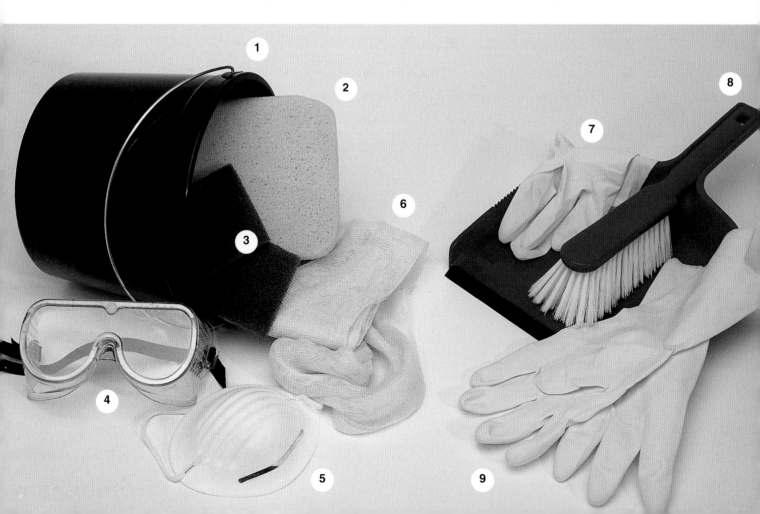

ADHESIVES

Mosaic suppliers carry an array of specialty glues for the various types of tesserae and surfaces involved in creating a mosaic work. When selecting an adhesive, make sure it is suitable for both the tesserae and the base of the mosaic. For indoor projects, tile mastic is a great choice because it is available in a premixed paste and is very strong. It may not hold up in a harsh winter climate, however. For outdoor projects, cement is the best choice because of its durability and strength. It needs to be mixed from powder and specially prepared to make it weatherproof (see Mixing Cement & Grout, below). Finally, when bonding glass tiles to a glass surface, a clear-drying adhesive specially formulated for the purpose is necessary to preserve translucency.

CEMENT & GROUT

Cement is often used as an adhesive in mosaic work because it is durable, reliable, and inexpensive. Use it for both indoor and especially outdoor projects. Grout, used to fill the spaces between tiles, adds to the strength and durability of a piece and is available in many colors and types. It can be purchased premixed, but the powdered form is very easy to use and is less expensive. Always follow the manufacturer's directions for mixing and using cement, grout, and additives and for applying grout sealant.

Many of the projects in this book call for sanded grout, which lends itself to mosaic work because it simulates textured grouting often found in traditional mosaics. It also complements the inherently dimensional surface of mosaic work, adding to its tactile beauty. Unsanded grout, such as the kind used for tiled bathroom floors, provides a smooth, caulk-like finish.

MIXING CEMENT & GROUT

Mix powdered cement and grout in small batches as needed, and always wear rubber gloves. Both cement and grout mixtures should be loose, spreadable pastes, but not too runny. Add the powder slowly to a small amount of water, mixing thoroughly, and continue to add powder until you achieve a fudge-like consistency. Once cement or grout is mixed, it should be used quickly before it becomes too dry.

For outdoor projects, use cement and grout formulated for outdoor use – they contain an acrylic additive, which provides extra strength. To guarantee lasting durability, mix the powder with a weatherproofing acrylic admixture, instead of water. The plastic nature of this additive prevents grout and cement from cracking when the mosaic is subjected to winter's freeze-thaw cycle. To be safe, cover outdoor pieces with plastic or bring them in during harsh or snowy weather.

Basic Mosaic Design

CREATING A DESIGN

Mosaic designs usually start with a personal theme or a particularly inspiring material, such as a gorgeous, but broken, china teapot. Perhaps there is a favorite chipped mug lingering in the cupboard that can be restored to usefulness as a coaster, or a damaged ceramic casserole cover with a vegetable motif that can be reused as a focal point in a framed piece for the kitchen.

CHOOSING A BASE

Another good way to come up with a design is to begin with a surface or a base for the mosaic. Is there a table, a birdbath, or an old flowerpot that is in need of refurbishing? These are all great items to begin with. After selecting a base, choose a color scheme according to where the piece will go. A flowerpot in shades of yellow and blue will brighten a dreary window; earth tones would look delicious covering a window box planted with kitchen herbs. Then, create a simple design for the mosaic inspired by the chosen base and colors.

FUNCTION AS INSPIRATION

The function of an item will often inspire a design as well. Picture water bubbling over the trout in the rain catcher on page 92, and it's obvious that the design works on many levels. Use it at a seaside cottage, and it's found the perfect home! Similarly, the stepping stones on page 72 are inspired by the bright, bold flowers of high summer. The simple, stylized design captures the multiple-petal beauty of many flowers, without replicating them exactly. This is the secret to a successful design! Don't be afraid to be too simplistic. Mosaics are inherently detailed and textured, and a simple design will enhance the beauty of the tiles and the workmanship.

TURNING A SKETCH INTO A PATTERN

First, begin with a hand-drawn sketch or a photocopy of a picture. For small works, the pattern can be easily drawn at actual size. For large pieces, such as a floor, the design needs to be scaled to the size of the mosaic surface. Sketching the design on graph paper or a grid will help set guidelines. For very large pieces, use a photocopier to enlarge the pattern in sections to the necessary size.

CREATING COLOR GUIDES

A sketch can also be simplified by outlining it on tracing paper, making it easier to transfer and read. Photocopy the outline on white paper and experiment with different color combinations, using pencils or markers. Having a colored pattern to refer to while working is extremely helpful, especially with very large pieces that have many colors and images. Then, cut out and trace the pattern on the mosaic base using a permanent marker or pencil. It is also helpful to sketch in colors or a numbering system directly on the base, to more easily distinguish which tiles go where.

This design, inspired by a traditional fifteenth-century mosaic, was updated for the classical entryway project on page 46. Since it will eventually be covered up, don't be afraid to draw the pattern directly on the surface to make applying tiles easier.

How to Cut Tiles

BREAKING CHINA & CERAMIC TILE

Many of the projects in this book make use of shards rather than perfectly trimmed tiles, which is a great way to recycle beautiful ceramics. To break whole dishes, cups, or large tiles, use a hammer. First, wrap the pieces to be smashed in a towel to prevent shards from being scattered, and always wear safety goggles. Then, use tile nippers to refine the shape of the pieces as necessary to fit them into a mosaic. To keep an image on patterned ceramic pieces intact, try to break them into a few very large pieces, then trim around the design with tile nippers and/or chipper nippers.

MAKING STRAIGHT CUTS

Use a combination scorer and plier to make straight cuts. It is important to apply firm, even pressure while scoring. Use a metal ruler to prevent the scorer from slipping and to keep the line perfectly straight. Then, grasp the tile with the tool and align the scoring with the guide mark, or the center of the tool's mouth. Press the handles together slowly and firmly, and the tile will snap off along the score mark.

SHAPING TILES

Once tiles have been broken or cut to the approximate size needed, additional shaping may be necessary to fit pieces into a mosaic. Use chipper nippers, which act as mosaic scissors, to cut away tiny bits of tile. Don't try to cut too much at once; rather, chip away at the tile, going over the same area a few times. Use this technique to make rounded or curved tiles, too. With a bit of practice, a variety of unusual and interesting shapes are possible. Try making ovals, hearts, or leaf-shaped tiles.

1 HAMMER AND SHARDS
Use a hammer to break china and ceramic ware into useable shards and then refine the pieces with a tile nipper.

2 TRIANGULAR TILES AND TOOL
Any kind of tile can be cut into several pieces with a scorer and plier and used for mosaic work.

3 ROUNDED TILES
Both glass and ceramic tiles can be further refined and shaped by using chipper nippers. Even teardrops and circles are possible!

4 GLASS TRIANGLES AND TILES
Glass can be cut just as easily as ceramics using the same techniques.

1

2

3

4

How to Lay Out a Pattern

The first thing to remember about assembling a mosaic is that the more closely tiles are placed together, the more solid the design will look; if the tiles are spaced more widely apart, the design will appear fractured. An intricate design, such as one that illustrates a scene, should have closely spaced tiles; but a geometric floor mosaic would look stunning with wider grout lines.

DIRECT TILE APPLICATION

There are two ways to apply tiles to a surface. The *direct method* involves placing tiles one by one, face up, on the base. This method can be used to apply tesserae to both rounded and flat surfaces and is good for any small project. Beginners should be sure to choose a rigid surface to work on, because any flexibility could cause the grout to crack or the tiles to pop off.

INDIRECT TILE APPLICATION

The *indirect method* involves placing tesserae face down on a temporary base, such as adhesive vinyl, then laying the tiles all at once onto a base covered with adhesive. This method is helpful when trying to achieve a flat surface, such as a floor, tabletop, or wall, or when working with flat, even tiles. Always make sure the surface is strong enough to support the weight of the tiles, grout, and adhesive, which can become extremely heavy.

For intricate or tricky areas of a design, use a chipper nipper to cut the tiles. Any oddly shaped or curved tesserae will need to be shaped carefully to ensure that they fit smoothly into the mosaic. Chipper nippers are specially designed for more precise cutting than tile nippers. Chip carefully and slowly away, checking the tiles against the pattern often and making adjustments as needed. If necessary, mark the tiles with a grease-pencil guideline.

The tiles used for the framed kitchen mosaic on page 42 had corner decorations that were reassembled to make the blue floral accents throughout the piece. When working with patterned ceramic shards, play with the pieces to discover interesting ways to rearrange the images. Tiles that extend past the edge of the mosaic, like the accent at the top of this frame, make a composition more dynamic.

Making Mosaics on Wood

Wood is the perfect choice for a custom-made mosaic base, such as the house-number plaque on page 100. Particle board and plywood are inexpensive, easy-to-use materials that can be cut to any shape with a jigsaw. Lumberyards and home-improvement centers will cut wood to the desired shape and size as well.

Any wooden item can be used, but if it has been varnished or painted, use coarse sandpaper to remove as much of the finish as possible. A sealer and primer may also be necessary to make sure that the mosaic adhesive bonds properly with the wood. A solution of white craft glue or carpenter's wood glue and water works well. Used furniture, frames, and unfinished items are all great choices for a mosaic base.

Wood is one of the most versatile materials for mosaic bases because it is comparatively lightweight, is available in a variety of thicknesses, has a porous surface, is easily customizable, and is generally easy to work with. However, wood will warp over time if left outdoors. Bring wood-based mosaics inside during harsh weather, and don't use wood for patio tabletops.

Making Mosaics on Cement

Cement bases work well for outdoor projects because they are inherently durable and weather resistant. Use cement prepared for outdoor use as the adhesive for any cement-based project that needs to be weather resistant (see page 15 for guidance). Check the local garden or home center for paving stones, flower-bed edgers, garden sculpture, and other cement items for inspiration. Pavers are available in many shapes, such as octagons and circles. Cement board, which is available at home-improvement centers, provides a flat, strong, durable surface for tabletops, floors, or wall panels.

When working with a cement base, be sure to clean it thoroughly first with soap and water. Then, let it dry completely before beginning the mosaic. Dust and grime can interfere with the adhesive bond.

Cement floors are also a suitable base for mosaic application, but it's best to have them professionally cleaned and prepared, especially if they are old or abused. Any paint will need to be removed, and all cracks should be filled.

This ordinary window box is just one of the many wooden items that provide a suitable surface for mosaic. The easy-to-draw-on surface makes transferring patterns a breeze. See page 68 for project instructions.

This old stone is soon to be transformed with an elegant stained-glass sun mosaic. The flat, small surface makes this project a perfect introduction to mosaics. See page 72 for instructions.

Making Mosaics on Metal

Any metal object can be used in mosaic work. Try refurbishing rusty garden furniture or transforming yard-sale finds. Mailboxes, doorknockers, shelf brackets, and wastebaskets would all make interesting and unusual surfaces for mosaic work. Try turning a coffee can into a decorative container, or turning a simple steel mixing bowl into a birdbath.

To prepare a metal surface for mosaic, first remove any rust with steel wool. The smooth surface of new metal items needs to be roughed up in order to take the adhesive properly, so give the entire piece a rubdown with steel wool until it feels coarse. Otherwise, the tiles may slip and slide, especially on curved surfaces.

This standard metal mailbox was decorated with flat-backed glass jewels, which are used whole rather than cut to fit. Cement is a good adhesive to use with metal bases, especially on outdoor projects. See page 102 for project instructions.

Making Mosaics on Glass

The variety of glass objects suitable for mosaics is staggering, and when paired with glass tiles, a luminous result is inevitable. Take advantage of the translucency of glass by decorating candle shades, votives, electric lampshades, or suncatchers. Old window panes, still in their frames, and vases are also good choices for mosaic work.

Always use glass cleaner and a lint-free cloth to prepare the surface. Fingerprints or oil from hands will interfere with the adhesive bond. Equally important is to use clear-drying adhesive specially formulated for glass. This will ensure that the translucency of the glass is uninhibited and that the adhesive is not visible from behind the tiles.

Since glass is translucent, keep in mind how the back of the project will be viewed. Be sure grout doesn't settle behind the tiles, as this will be visible from the front and the back. A good way to avoid this is to use enough adhesive to bond the entire surface area of each tile, but not so much that it oozes up into the grout lines. Practice on a scrap of glass first, to determine how much adhesive is necessary.

An ordinary mailbox can be the perfect storage container for garden tools. Covered with multicolor glass beads, this box will sparkle in the sunlight.

Electric patio lights can be turned into elegant stained-glass shades, which filter light beautifully. A string of lights enhances the effect by filling a whole space with colored light; it's well worth the effort. See page 64 for instructions.

USING COLOR EFFECTIVELY

The use of color in a mosaic has a profound effect on the overall mood and feeling of the piece. Consider not only the colors of the tiles, but the color of the grout as well. If colors are too contrasting, the design may become choppy and lose focus; if the colors are too similar, detail can be lost.

When selecting colors, many things should be taken into consideration to successfully render a mosaic design. Ask the following questions to determine what factors or results are most important:

Should the piece convey a relaxing or energetic feeling?
Will the mosaic be placed indoors or outdoors?
What sort of light will the mosaic be viewed in?
Are the mosaic images intended to be realistic or whimsical?
Is the mosaic inspired by a certain time period or artistic style?
Last, but certainly not least, what colors appeal to you personally?

COLOR SCHEMES

1 ORANGE, RED
Bright colors confer energy and vitality to their surroundings. Use them for bold, dynamic designs or to draw attention to a specific area of a mosaic.

2 EARTH TONES
Earth tones are comforting colors, ranging from brown to blue, red to green. Drawn from nature, they can't help but be harmonious when used together. Use them to seamlessly integrate a mosaic into the garden.

3 BLACK & WHITE STRIPE
Use black and white together for a classic, dramatic look. Since they are neutral, they can be used to easily accent other colors and are great for borders.

4 BLUES
A monochromatic palette can be intriguing and sophisticated when the boundaries of color are tested. A pattern of light-to dark-blue tiles is more interesting with a few teal tiles and gives the arrangement shading and depth.

5 PASTELS, PURPLE AND GREEN
Pastels are soft colors that can be worked into virtually any design, because they enhance brighter colors without detracting from them. Use them for a subdued, calming effect.

6 GREEN X AND ORANGE X WITH BLUE CENTER
The central blue tile in each of these arrangements shows how different a color can look depending on the hues surrounding it. True blue, paired with an orange of equal intensity, makes for a high-contrast color scheme. When surrounded by greens of equal intensity, the blue almost disappears.

7 SQUARES WITH BLUE TILES
Use several shades of the same color to add depth to a monotone arrangement. This technique can be used to create an interesting background pattern that enhances the focal point of a design without detracting from it.

8 WHITE T'S SURROUNDED BY BLUE AND GREEN
To make patterns, and especially letters, stand out, try outlining them with a darker or lighter color. The outline has to be sufficiently contrasting to be effective, as in the blue-and-white example here.

9 GREEN WITH RED STRIPE; RED WITH DARKER RED STRIPE
Complementary colors, such as green and red, appear to vibrate or flicker when placed together. Yellow-purple and blue-orange combinations also share this characteristic. Use a lighter shade of either color to minimize the vibrating effect, which can be distracting. Use shades of the same color for minimal contrast.

10 ROW OF 4 SQUARES WITH X'S IN THE MIDDLE
The same design can be highly defined or subdued, depending on the colors involved. Play with highly contrasting and minimally contrasting designs to see what works best.

CHOOSING GROUT COLORS

In a mosaic, the color of the grout is just as important as the color of the tiles. Grout lines can pull a range of colors together, highlight or minimize the fragmented feel of a piece, or be barely visible. The color of grout that should be used in a piece depends entirely on the desired effect. Make a few thumbnail mosaics using the same kinds of tiles in the original, then experiment with different grout colors.

In general, the more the grout color contrasts with the overall color scheme of the mosaic, the more visible and fragmented the piece will look. The more closely the grout matches the overall color scheme, the more unified the piece will look. Try combining different grout colors in the same piece to highlight or subdue certain areas.

These palettes, which range from warm-to cool-colored tiles, also show various grouting styles. Use them as a handy reference for the moods and effects possible by combining different grout and tile colors.

Delicate china patterns pair well with the simplicity and purity of white grout. See page 104 for instructions.

To make bright colors pop, outline them with black grout. See page 68 for instructions.

1 UNGROUTED PANEL

The farther apart the spaces between the tiles in an ungrouted mosaic are, the more unfinished and broken the piece will look. If tiles are placed very close together, the design will read well. Smalti are traditionally left ungrouted because the pitted and uneven surface traps grout, causing the handmade glass to become dulled. Instead, the tiles are pushed into a bed of adhesive such as cement, which partially fills the spaces between them.

2 BLACK GROUTED PANEL

Black grout accentuates the brighter colors in this palette and gives the whole panel a leaded, stained-glass feel. The shapes of the yellow shards are clearly defined, while the darker purple and blue tiles meld together.

3 WHITE GROUTED PANEL

White grout is useful for pieces with light or pale color schemes. With bright, dark, and medium-toned colors, white grout highlights the shape of each tile, giving the piece a fragmented feeling.

4 GRAY GROUTED PALETTE

Gray grout was used on this palette. The rainbow of color is pulled together into a harmonious whole by the neutral, soft gray grout lines, which are obvious but not overpowering. This grout also looks like cement, which works well for outdoor projects like birdbaths. For the most harmonious look when a mosaic incorporates a wide range of colors, use a grout that is neither too dark nor too light, or for less harmony, use different colors of grout in each area.

1

2

3

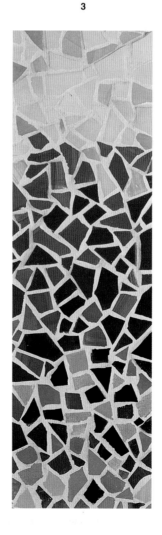

4

Mosaics Inside

Artist: Twyla Arthur
Photo by Twyla Arthur

cement board

stone or porcelain ceramic tiles, all the same thickness

black and white tiles for the border

palette knife

heavy-duty utility knife

hammer

tile nippers

cement

sanded gray grout

large sponge

safety goggles

latex gloves

filter mask

mixing bowls for cement and grout

Playroom Floor

This truck features marble headlights, which are sure to delight children

and adults alike. Simple, fun touches like these marbles make a mosaic

engaging, and that is certainly a welcome quality in a child's playroom.

Choose simple, easy-to-recognize designs, such as a rainbow or an animal,

or just bright geometric shapes. Encourage the kids to help by choosing the

pattern or placing some of the tiles themselves!

Illustrator: Mary Newell DePalma

STARTING OUT   A section of the original floor will need to be removed in order to place the mosaic. Consult with a contractor about the best way to do this. Prepare a pattern by sizing the illustration to your selected tabletop. You can enlarge the pattern in sections using a copier, or sketch or photocopy the illustration onto graph paper to determine scale.

STEP 1   Wearing safety goggles and protective gloves, break the ceramics to be used into large shards using a hammer (see page 20 for guidance). Then, cut the cement board to the desired size by deeply scoring it using a ruler and heavy-duty utility knife. Snap the excess off by simply aligning the scorings with the edge of a table and applying pressure to the pieces that extend past the table's edge. Next, cut each design element out of paper and trace around it with a permanent marker to transfer the pattern directly onto the cement board. Use 4-inch (10-cm) by 4-inch (10-cm) or 6-inch (15-cm) by 6-inch (15-cm) whole tiles for the border.

Tip: The stone used here measures 3/4 inch (2 cm) thick. For beginners, high-fire or porcelain tiles of the same thickness are easier to work with. They come in a variety of colors and are strong enough to withstand the wear and tear of children playing.

STEP 2   Prepare the cement for indoor use (see page 15 for guidance). Using a flexible palette knife, spread the perimeter of the board with a 1/8-inch (3-mm) layer of cement and begin applying the black and white border tiles. Leave out four tiles for screw holes so that the floor can be easily installed. Fill in the rest of the design according to the pattern, spreading cement over a 6-inch (15-cm) to 8-inch (20-cm) -square area at a time. Finally, apply the marble headlights, using extra cement for a secure bond. Let it dry for twenty-four hours.

Prepare gray sanded grout for indoor use (see page 15), then begin spreading it over an 8-inch (20-cm) to 10-inch (25-cm) area of the floor with glove-protected hands. Work the grout completely into the crevices between the shards using a circular motion. Continue until all the spaces between the shards are filled. Keep wiping excess grout off the surface of the shards. When the grout has dried enough to become powdery, no more than fifteen to twenty minutes, use a large damp sponge to clean the tiles. Rinse the sponge frequently, and wipe the tiles until all the grout film is gone. Buff with a dry cloth when the grout is completely dry. Let the floor dry for a week before installation.

To install the floor, use flat-headed screws in the empty spaces and make sure they are flush with the surface of the board. Next, apply tiles to cover the spaces. Let it dry twenty-four hours, then grout.

VARIATION

The timeless appeal of a rainbow motif is perfect for a playroom floor. The simple pattern seen here is a great starting point for beginning mosaicists, because it can be easily drawn and laid out. Follow the directions for the main project to ensure the floor's durability.

Illustrator: Mary Newell DePalma

Materials

framed mirror

broken ceramic dishes

palette knife

hammer

screws

tile nippers

tile mastic

white sanded grout

kitchen scrubbing pad

cloth towel

safety goggles

latex gloves

filter mask

mixing bowls for cement
and grout

Artist: Doreen Mastandrea

Ceramic Relief Mirror

A framed mirror of any size can be used for this project. Choose one that has an interesting shape, then select ceramic pieces that will accentuate it. Beautiful, handmade plates with a dimensional rope pattern were used here to outline the scalloped border at the top of the frame. Take advantage of curved plate edges to create striking rounded borders.

Experiment with different ways of arranging the shards by laying them out on a piece of paper next to the frame. There is no need to plan out the entire frame, but it is helpful to work out the focal points beforehand.

STEP 1

Wearing safety goggles and protective gloves, break the ceramics to be used into shards using a hammer (see page 20 for guidance). Try to keep interesting designs intact by using tile nippers to extract them safely from large, broken pieces.

Tip: Having a variety of shapes and sizes of ceramic pieces on hand will make it faster and easier to fill the space on the frame and will add interest to the design.

STEP 2

With a palette knife, spread a 1/8-inch (3-mm) -thick layer of mastic on approximately 6 inches (15 cm) of the frame. Start applying shards side by side until you cover the area. Spread on more mastic and continue applying shards all the way around the frame. If you decide to cover the edges of the frame, be careful because this is a delicate area and shards may chip off over time. You can grout or paint the edges instead after the mosaic is completed. Let it dry for twenty-four hours.

Tip: Be careful not to apply too much mastic, because the excess will be displaced into the spaces between the tiles, leaving little room for grout.

STEP 3

Prepare grout for indoor use (see page 15), then apply a small amount on the frame with glove-protected hands. Work the grout completely into the crevices between the shards using a circular motion. Fill all the spaces between the shards. Continue wiping excess grout off the surface of the shards, because it will be difficult to sand off once dry. When the grout has dried enough to become powdery, no more than fifteen to twenty minutes, use a dry kitchen scrubbing pad to sand excess grout off the surface of the shards. Wear a filter mask while sanding. If the scrubbing pad scratches the glaze, wipe off excess grout while it is wet with a damp sponge, let it dry, then buff with a lint-free rag.

Tip: If the grout has not dried enough before sanding, the scrubbing pad will get saturated with moist grout. If this happens, wait a little longer before trying again with a dry pad.

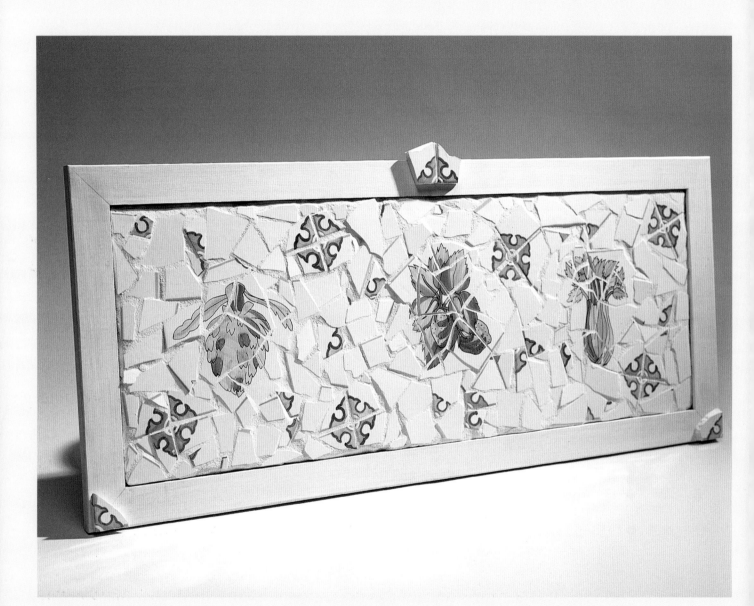

Artist: Aimee Southworth

Materials

- wood-backed frame
- decorative kitchen tiles
- palette knife
- hammer
- tile nippers
- tile mastic
- white sanded grout
- kitchen scrubbing pad
- safety goggles
- latex gloves
- filter mask
- mixing bowls for cement and grout

Framed Kitchen Mosaic

This framed project is an easy way to incorporate mosaic art into any space – just customize the size, shape, and theme to match a particular decor. With the variety of decorated tiles available, almost any pattern is possible! When breaking tiles, keep special designs whole, or try combining shards in new ways to make innovative patterns. The blue flowers in this design were made using four corner pieces from the tiles used here.

STARTING OUT   Retrofit any store-bought frame for this project by nailing a thin piece of
wood to the back. Then, paint the frame if desired and let it dry completely
before beginning the mosaic.

STEP 1

Wearing safety goggles and protective gloves,
break the ceramics to be used into large shards
using a hammer (see page 20 for guidance). Use
tile nippers to cut around designs, such as the
vegetables here, and keep them together.

STEP 2

With a palette knife, spread the backs of shards
with a 1/8-inch (3-mm) -thick layer of mastic.
Begin applying shards that need to be placed in
specific areas first, then fill in the rest of the
space using solidly colored, plain remnants from
the decorative tiles. Here, the three vegetable
motifs were applied first and spaced evenly
apart. Let it dry for twenty-four hours.

**Tip: Use a piece of paper cut to the same size as the frame to
plan the placement of the tiles before applying them.**

**Tip: When using mastic, try not to move tiles that have
already been applied; any movement before drying will
weaken the bond.**

VARIATION

Use cement board, available at hardware stores, and a lettering stencil to make a weatherproof sign like the one seen here. First, cut the board to the desired size by deeply scoring it using a ruler and heavy-duty utility knife, then snap the excess off. To do this, simply align the scored edges with the edge of a table, then apply pressure to the pieces that extend past the table's edge. Next, trace the lettering using a permanent marker directly on the cement board. Try making a custom alphabet for tracing with a computer and printer.

Artist: Doreen Mastandrea

Apply the lettering tiles first, then complete the border, and finally fill the remaining background areas. The vitreous glass tiles on this sign were applied using cement mixed for outdoor use. Be sure to also use grout mixed for outdoor use (see page 15 for guidance). Finally, apply grout sealant according to the manufacturer's directions.

STEP 3

Prepare white sanded grout for indoor use (see page 15 for guidance), then apply a small amount on the mosaic with glove-protected hands. Work the grout completely into the crevices between the shards using a circular motion, or use a rubber spatula if the shards are flat and of the same thickness. Fill all the spaces between the shards. Continue wiping excess grout off the surface of the shards. When the grout has dried enough to become powdery, no more than fifteen to twenty minutes, use a dry kitchen scrubbing pad to sand excess grout off the surface of the shards. Wear a filter mask while sanding. If the scrubbing pad scratches the glaze, wipe off excess grout while it is wet with a damp sponge, let it dry, then buff with a lint-free rag.

Tip: If there are any large, hard-to-remove spots of grout that have dried on the tiles, use a craft knife to scrape them off.

Artist: Doreen Mastandrea
Photo by: Regina Grenier

cement board

ceramic tiles or shards

palette knife

heavy-duty utility knife

hammer

tile nippers

cement

grout

acrylic admixture

kitchen scrubbing pad

safety goggles

Classical Entryway

This entryway was inspired by traditional mosaic designs but is made with broken ceramic tiles instead of handmade glass smalti for a modern appeal. When planning a design, take into consideration the colors and the lighting of the room where the floor will be installed. Vary the colors of images within the pattern to create added detail and depth. The grapes here incorporate several shades of red and maroon, and the foliage is made with several shades of green. Many copy shops will enlarge a pattern to scale, which makes it easier to transfer the design. This mosaic measures 3 feet (91 cm) by 4 feet (122 cm).

STARTING OUT Cement board, available at hardware stores, is used to make a durable base for this entryway. Make sure that the subfloor is sufficiently stable; consult with a contractor if you are unsure. If the subfloor has any flex to it, the tiles will also flex and eventually pop out. To use the board, first cut it to the desired size by deeply scoring it using a ruler and heavy-duty utility knife. Then, snap the excess off by simply aligning the scorings with the edge of a table and applying pressure to the pieces that extend past the table's edge.

STEP 1

Wearing safety goggles and protective gloves, break the ceramics to be used into large shards using a hammer (see page 20 for guidance). Use tile nippers to cut the shards into smaller pieces for the images and the vines. Use the larger pieces for the background. Next, cut each design element out of paper and trace around it with a permanent marker to transfer the pattern directly on the cement board. Alternatively, try using graphite paper, usually found in art and craft supply stores, to transfer the design. Slip a sheet under the pattern, then trace over the lines of the photocopy. Because graphite paper only comes in 8 1/2-inch by 11-inch sheets, it will not be large enough to transfer a design 3 feet by 4 feet. So, you will need to transfer the design bit by bit by moving the graphite paper around to each area.

STEP 2

Prepare the cement for outdoor use (see page 15 for guidance). Using a flexible palette knife, spread a small area of the board with a 1/8-inch (3-mm) layer of cement, then begin applying the shards. Start with shards that need to be placed in specific areas, such as the vines, leaves, and grapes seen here, then fill in the rest of the background. Leave several empty spaces for screw holes so that the floor can be easily and securely installed. Finally, complete the border. Let it dry for twenty-four hours.

Tip: When selecting tiles for this project, be sure to test the durability of the glaze with a kitchen scrubbing pad. If it gets scratched easily, consider using other ceramics.

Tip: A large mosaic such as this one requires many tiles. When using ceramic shards, double-check that there are enough of each color and pattern to complete the project before beginning it.

Try making a special frame for a mosaic picture
by experimenting with different motifs and
colors borrowed from the main design. This
border uses purple and green from the entryway to create a repeating, stylized grape-leaf
pattern. To help define the pattern further, two
colors of grout are used – midnight blue around
the leaves, and terra cotta within them.

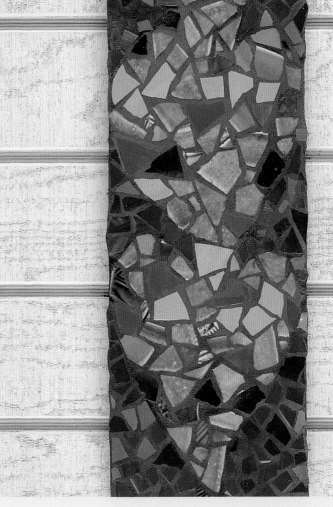

STEP 3

Prepare grout for outdoor use (see page 15),
then begin spreading it over one-third of the floor
with glove-protected hands. Work the grout completely into the crevices between the shards
using a circular motion. Continue until all the
spaces between the shards are filled. Keep wiping excess grout off the surface of the shards.
When the grout has dried enough to become
powdery, no more than fifteen to twenty minutes,
use a large damp sponge to clean the tiles. Rinse
the sponge frequently, and wipe the tiles until all
the grout film is gone. When the grout is completely dry, buff with a dry cloth. Then, complete
another third of the floor in the same way and,
finally, the last third. Let the floor mosaic dry for
a week before installation.

To install the entryway, use flat-headed screws in
the empty spaces and make sure they are flush
with the surface of the board. Next, apply tiles
to cover the heads of the screws. Let it dry for
twenty-four hours, then grout.

Materials   hooks

plywood board

yellow ceramic shards

polka-dot pieces

solid blue tiles

palette knife

hammer

screwdriver

screws

tile nippers

tile mastic

white sanded grout

kitchen scrubbing pad

safety goggles

latex gloves

filter mask

mixing bowls for cement and grout

Wall Hook Rack

Patterned ceramics provide an inspiring array of decorative elements

that can be used to great effect in mosaic work. Images can be broken

Artist: Doreen Mastandrea apart at random and rearranged or carefully broken out and kept whole.

In the rack seen here, solid blue, dotted blue, and yellow ceramic tiles

were used to match these decorative ball hooks perfectly. Alternatively,

try selecting ceramic pieces with interesting designs, then find hooks

that complement them.

Plan the arrangement of the patterned shards on the rack before applying them, especially if there is a limited supply. They should be spaced out somewhat evenly, so that one area of the rack does not seem to have more than another.

STEP 1

Wearing safety goggles and protective gloves, break the ceramics to be used into shards using a hammer (see page 20 for guidance). Use tile nippers to refine the size and shape of the shards as necessary. To make the rack, cut a piece of plywood to the desired size, then attach the hooks to the board with screws.

STEP 2

Spread the back of four polka-dot shards with a 1/8-inch (3-mm) -thick layer of mastic, and apply them so they are partly running off the four corners of the board. This is a visually playful way of breaking up the rectangular shape of the rack. Next, randomly apply the yellow shards and some polka-dot shards on all parts of the rack, spaced somewhat evenly apart. Then, spread mastic on a small area of the rack and apply solid blue shards. Continue until the rack is covered. The tile nippers can be used to shape pieces for hard-to-reach areas around the hooks. Let it dry for twenty-four hours.

**Artists: Deb Mandile,
Dawn Dimadona, and
Doreen Mastandrea**

VARIATION

Make your own customized rack using antique hooks and plywood. Begin by cutting a piece of plywood to the desired size, then attach hooks to the board with screws. Next, select patterned ceramic pieces that match the shape, color, or decoration of the hooks. A broken ceramic lamp base with a swirl pattern was used here to complement these curved antique hooks. Follow the steps from the main project for applying the shards and grouting. The neutral gray grout used here is a perfect match for the black-and-white color scheme of the shards.

STEP 3

Prepare grout for indoor use (see page 15), then apply a small amount on the rack with glove-protected hands. If the shards are of a uniform thickness, try using a flexible rubber spatula to apply the grout. Work the grout completely into the crevices between the shards using a circular motion. Fill all the spaces between the shards. Continue wiping excess grout off the surface of the shards, because it will be difficult to sand off once dry. When the grout has dried enough to become powdery, no more than fifteen to twenty minutes, use a dry kitchen scrubbing pad to sand excess grout off the surface of the ceramic shards. Wear a filter mask while sanding. If the scrubbing pad scratches the glaze, wipe off excess grout while it is wet with a damp sponge, let it dry, then buff with a lint-free rag. Attach hardware to the back of the rack for hanging, if necessary.

Tip: Mount each hook on a small piece of plywood before attaching it to the board. This will raise the hooks up enough to accommodate the thickness of the shards that will cover the rack.

BITS & PIECES:
WORKING WITH GLASS

Glass was used to create many of the classic mosaics that adorn ancient buildings and cathedrals throughout Europe. The highly reflective, translucent, shimmering qualities of glass tiles can make a two-dimensional image spring to life, especially when viewed in a sunbathed spot. The vibrant color and tonal variation inherent in this material make it easy to create images with shading effects, giving pieces an illustrated look. Try using mirror or freeform sea glass with traditional tiles for an eclectic design.

1 VITREOUS GLASS TILES

Vitreous glass tiles come in a variety of colors, are easy to cut, and have a corrugated back to aid adhesion. All of these qualities make them a great option for beginners, as well as more experienced mosaicists. They are generally 3/4 inch by 3/4 inch by 3/16 inch (20 mm by 20 mm by 4 mm) and are sold by the pound or on sheets of paper. Their beveled edges also work well with three-dimensional and curved designs, and the flat upper surface makes them perfect for decorating tabletops and floors. Since they are weather resistant, they are also a good choice for outdoor mosaics.

2 GLASS BEADS

These flat-backed glass jewels come in many colors and sizes. They are generally transparent and bright and can be found at stained-glass supply stores as well as home centers. The natural shape of these beads makes it easy to incorporate round elements into a design, rather than trying to cut circular tiles.

3 MARBLES

Marbles of all kinds can be used in a mosaic. Because they are completely round, pay special attention when applying them. Use extra adhesive, and place them last, if possible, to minimize the possibility of knocking them loose.

4 STAINED GLASS

Stained-glass pieces are spectacular on mosaics that will be viewed in a sunny spot. Cut custom tiles from sheets of glass, or ask a stained-glass artist about their scraps. They will usually have an abundance of shards in a variety of textures, shapes, and colors.

5 METALLIC VITREOUS GLASS

Vitreous glass tiles are also available with metallic finishes or inclusions, which add a luxurious feeling to any design. These are dappled with flecks of gold.

6 SMALTI TILES

These Italian tiles are made of opaque glass and are the classic material used for mosaics. Sold in approximately 1/8-inch by 1/2-inch by 1/4-inch (10-mm by 15-mm by 7-mm) rectangles, they have an irregular and highly reflective surface that catches light beautifully. Because of their uneven surface, smalti mosaics are usually left ungrouted, so that the pits and recesses do not become filled with grout. Traditionally, smalti are pressed into a bed of mortar. The mortar is consequently pushed into the crevices between the tiles, creating a grouted look. Smalti are ideal for walls and decorative pieces rather than projects requiring a flat, finished surface like floors.

4

5

6

Mosaics Outside

**Artist: Linda
Benswanger/Mozayiks
Photo by Allen Bryan**

Materials
- marine board
- wrought iron base
- broken ceramic pieces
- palette knife
- hammer
- tile nippers
- cement
- natural gray or dark gray sanded grout
- acrylic admixture
- grout sealant
- kitchen scrubbing pad
- safety goggles
- latex gloves
- filter mask
- mixing bowls for cement and grout

Wrought Iron Patio Table

This elegant wrought iron table is a welcome addition to the garden, creating an ideal place to sit, eat, or just reflect. Sketch out ideas and plan the design on paper first, using colors, themes, or plantings from the garden as inspiration. Since this is a large project, tailor the design to fit skill level as well as personal taste so that it doesn't become overwhelming. The custom table here is made from a marine-board top and a separate base. Marine board, which resists warping, can be found at home-improvement centers. A whole wrought iron or metal patio table with a solid top can also be used for this project.

Artist: Linda Benswanger/Mozayiks

STARTING OUT

Attach the marine-board tabletop to the base before beginning the mosaic, because it will be much lighter and easier to manipulate. First, cut the board with a jigsaw or have a piece custom cut at a lumberyard or home center. Then, drill holes through the board that correspond with screw holes in the table base. Holes can be drilled into the base, if necessary, with a metal-cutting drill bit. Prepare a pattern by sizing the illustration to your selected tabletop. You can enlarge the pattern in sections using a copier, or sketch or photocopy the illustration onto graph paper to determine scale.

STEP 1

First, trace the pattern onto the marine board with a pencil or marker. Then, wearing safety goggles and protective gloves, break the ceramics to be used into shards using a hammer (see page 20 for guidance). Small to medium-size pieces, about 1/2 inch (1 cm) or 2 inches (5 cm), will work well for this project. Keep colors separated for quicker and easier application. Use tile nippers to refine the size and shape of the shards as necessary.

Tip: Use flat tiles to ensure that the tabletop has an even surface. Tile stores will often sell broken or discontinued merchandise at a discount.

STEP 2

Prepare the cement for outdoor use (see page 15). Use a flexible palette knife to apply a 1/8-inch (3-mm) layer of cement over a 6-inch (15-cm) -square area. Begin applying tiles, and continue until the entire horizontal surface is covered. Then, apply tiles to the vertical edges of the table. Let it dry for twenty-four hours.

Tip: Code each section of the pattern with a colored marker or numbering system, then complete one section before moving on to the next. This will eliminate confusion and make the process quicker.

Prepare grout for outdoor use (see page 15), then apply a small amount to the table with glove-protected hands. Work the grout completely into the crevices between the tiles using a circular motion. Keep wiping excess grout off the surface of the tiles. When the grout has dried enough to become powdery, no more than fifteen to twenty minutes, use a damp sponge to clean the tiles. Rinse the sponge frequently, and wipe the tiles until all the grout film is gone. Let it dry, then buff with a rag. When the grout is completely dry, which will take a few days, depending on humidity, apply grout sealant according to the manufacturer's directions.

Tip: When grouting the sides of the table, be sure to cover the bottoms of the tiles to conceal any sharp edges.

Tip: To prevent the table's horizontal surface from collecting snow or ice, bring it inside in winter or cover it with a tarp.

VARIATION

Play with the colors for this geometric design by spreading out several ceramic samples, then freely mix and match them. For an outdoor table such as this one, choose a sunny location for viewing the samples, because indoor lighting can cause certain colors to appear warmer or cooler than they really are. Be sure to follow the directions for the main project to ensure the durability of your outdoor table.

Illustrator: Mary Newell DePalma

Materials

- hanging light with glass shade
- opaque and translucent stained glass
- wooden craft stick
- glass cutter
- grease pencil
- craft knife
- sand paper
- clean cotton rags
- clear adhesive for bonding glass to glass
- navy or black sanded grout
- acrylic admixture
- safety goggles
- latex gloves
- filter mask
- mixing bowls for cement and grout

Glass Patio Lights

**Artist: Linda
Benswanger/Mozayiks**

Reminiscent of stained-glass lamps, these glass patio lights can set a festive, romantic, or soothing mood, depending on the color of the tiles that cover the shade. Use only glass shades to ensure the most brilliant, sparkling light. A variety of prewired shades, such as the ones seen here, can be found at home centers and lighting stores. The easy-to-cut custom tiles used in this project are made from sheets of stained glass using one simple tool.

STARTING OUT Since both the shade and the tiles are transparent, it is very important to use adhesive specially made for bonding glass to glass that dries clear. Ask for it at the local hardware store.

STEP 1 Wearing safety goggles and sturdy work gloves to protect hands from sharp edges, cut the glass into square and rectangular tiles using a glass cutter. First, use a ruler and a grease pencil to measure and mark the glass for cutting. Then, use firm, even pressure to score the glass with the cutter along the first line. Next, lightly tap the glass along the scoring with the end of the cutter, and gently snap the glass into two pieces. It should break along the scored line. Repeat the procedure until all the tiles are cut. After cutting the glass, it is helpful to sort the pieces by color.

STEP 2 Squeeze some glass adhesive on a piece of cardboard or a plate. With a wooden craft stick, spread a 6-inch (15-cm) area of the shade with adhesive, and spread a small amount on the back of the tile. Begin applying the tiles. Cover the entire shade, fitting the pieces together very tightly to ensure maximum luminosity and a minimum of grout. Let it dry for twenty-four hours.

Tip: Use opaque or semi-opaque glass tiles for this project, which will conceal any grout that may have settled behind them.

Tip: If the glue is runny or very wet, let it dry to tackiness on the shade before applying the tiles.

VARIATION

Shades of all shapes can be decorated using the same technique described for the main project. Glass tiles in pastel colors were used on this shade to create a softer look.

 STEP 3 Prepare grout for outdoor use (see page 15), then spread a small amount on the shade with rubber glove – protected hands. Work the grout completely into the crevices between the tiles using a circular motion. Be careful to continually wipe excess grout off the tiles. Continue until all the spaces between the tiles are filled. Once the grout has dried enough to form a powdery film on the top of the glass tiles, use a dry rag to wipe off the film. Let the shade dry for twenty-four hours, then buff the glass with a clean cotton rag.

Tip: If there are any sharp edges sticking out of the grout after the project is completed, use a medium-grade sandpaper to remove them.

Materials

wooden window box

ceramic shards in earth tones

craft stick or plastic knife

hammer

tile nippers

tile mastic

rust-colored sanded grout

acrylic admixture

kitchen scrubbing pad

safety goggles

latex gloves

filter mask

mixing bowls for cement and grout

Three-Season Window Planter

Artists: Bruce Winn and Doreen Mastandrea

Undulating bands of color continue all the way around this planter, creating a dynamic design that keeps the eye moving without being distracting. The key to creating a harmonious design such as this one is to keep the pattern simple and distinct. Resist the temptation to add more detail — the completed mosaic will be greater than the sum of its parts. The base for this project is a simple pine window box, which can be purchased at home centers and garden stores. These planters should be sheltered in the winter to prevent splitting or cracking of the wood.

Earth tones, such as the moss green, butter yellow, and golden brown used here, enhance lush foliage and flowers alike. The red accents, reminiscent of berries, are sprinkled throughout the design to brighten up the planter.

STEP 1

Wearing safety goggles and protective gloves, break the ceramics to be used for the design and the border into shards using a hammer (see page 20 for guidance). Small pieces will work best for this intricate design. Separate the shards by color in bowls. Use tile nippers to refine the size and shape of the shards as necessary. Also nip very tiny accent pieces like the red ones used here.

STEP 2

Draw continuous, wavy lines around the planter to define the spaces for each color. Try sketching the design first, then finalizing it with a permanent marker. Mark spots for the red dots in an orderly pattern. Number each section of the pattern, and use this as a guide for applying the tiles in alternating bands of color. Each number should correspond to a different color. Then, with a palette knife, spread an area about 6 inches (15 cm) wide with a 1/8-inch (3-mm) -thick layer of tile mastic. Apply the blue border tiles to the top and bottom of the planter first, then apply tiny accent pieces. Next, begin filling in the wavy pattern, starting with color number one and continue until the planter is completed. Let dry for twenty-four hours.

Tip: It is easier to apply accents like these red dots first and work around them, rather than trying to fit them in last.

VARIATION

This whimsical, geometric planter uses black grout to make the brightly colored design pop. Use embellishments in the corners, like these ceramic spheres, to give the piece dimensionality. Follow the directions for the main project, but when adding the corner embellishments, be sure to use plenty of tile mastic for a strong, durable bond.

Artists: Michelle Fino, Carole Martin, and Doreen Mastandrea

STEP 3

Prepare rust-colored sanded grout for outdoor use (see page 15 for guidance), then apply a small amount on the planter with glove-protected hands. Work the grout completely into the crevices between the shards using a circular motion. Fill all the spaces between the shards. Continue wiping excess grout off the surface of the shards. When the grout has dried enough to become powdery, no more than fifteen to twenty minutes, use a dry kitchen scrubbing pad to sand excess grout off the surface of the shards. Wear a filter mask while sanding. If the scrubbing pad scratches the glaze, wipe off excess grout while it is wet with a damp sponge, let it dry, then buff with a lint-free rag.

Materials

square cement garden paver

stained glass, preferably opaque

palette knife or craft stick

tile nippers

combination scorer and pliers for cutting glass

cement

acrylic admixture

natural sanded grout

kitchen scrubbing pad

latex gloves

filter mask

mixing bowls for cement and grout

Sunshine Stepping Stones

**Artist: Linda
Benswanger/Mozayiks**

For almost immediate satisfaction, try making quick-and-easy stepping stones like these. Precast cement shapes for paving and edging are available at nearly any home-and-garden center and are relatively inexpensive. Use brightly colored glass tiles to keep the stones from fading into the background in an outdoor setting; they will sparkle in the sun. Make multiple stones and vary the images for a playful patio walkway, or use them as focal points in the garden – and even indoors as trivets or decorative accents!

STARTING OUT Wash the paver thoroughly to guarantee a strong bond with the cement adhesive. When dry, draw the pattern directly on the stone to eliminate guesswork when applying tiles.

STEP 1.

Cut the glass tiles using a combination scorer and pliers tool. First, score the section of glass to be cut, applying firm, even pressure. Then, grasp the glass with the tool and align the scoring with the guide mark. Press firmly, and the glass should snap off along the scoring. Keep the pieces organized as they are cut for easy installation by laying them out on a sketched paper pattern.

STEP 2

Prepare cement for outdoor use (see page 15 for guidance). Next, use a palette knife or craft stick to apply a 1/8-inch (3-mm) -thick layer of cement over a small area of the paver. Begin applying tiles, starting with the border. A simple alternating pattern of two colors was used here. Then, continue applying tiles, working from the center of the paver toward the border. Let it dry for twenty-four hours.

Tip: For a small, flat project such as this one, cut all the tiles needed before starting to apply them. Cut a few extra pieces, though, to avoid coming up short.

Tip: The defining, striped border here is highly visible in a garden setting. However, a looser pattern would still read well from a distance.

VARIATION

Cement borders, stepping stones, and pavers come in a variety of shapes and sizes. This scalloped border piece, intended to edge a flower bed, features a glass-tile floral pattern. The scalloped shape is a perfect accent for the soft, curving shape of many flowers. To make it, simply follow the directions for the garden paver. Experiment with simple and more intricate designs, and use colors that will complement nearby plantings.

STEP 3

Prepare natural sanded grout for outdoor use (see page 15), then apply a small amount to the paver with glove-protected hands. Work the grout completely into the crevices between the tiles using a circular motion. Continue until all the spaces between the tiles are filled. Keep wiping excess grout off the surface of the tiles. When the grout has dried enough to become powdery, no more than fifteen to twenty minutes, use a damp sponge to clean the tiles. Rinse the sponge frequently and wipe the tiles until all the grout film is gone. Finally, buff the glass with a dry cloth when the grout is completely dry.

BITS & PIECES:
WORKING WITH FOUND OBJECTS

Virtually anything can be used for mosaic work. Mosaic artists see the possibilities in everything around them, and often collect odds and ends such as buttons, mirrors, beads, jewelry, pendants, coins, and bottle tops to incorporate into their projects. These are just some of the unusual items that can be transformed into tesserae. The only limit is the artist's imagination. Collecting strange or striking objects becomes a habit for the adventurous mosaic enthusiast who delights in creating the unexpected! To spark ideas for how to create a picture using a random assortment of bits and pieces, play with them — sort them by color, shape, and texture.

1 METAL GRAPES
Cast metal pieces such as the grapes seen here add dimension to a mosaic. One uniquely shaped item can serve as the focal point of a piece, and inspire an entire project.

2 POTTERY SHARDS
Pottery shards offer a wide array of colors and motifs to choose from. Painted details can be broken apart and rearranged, or simply extracted and used whole.

3 ROUND GLASS BEADS
Inexpensive, flatbacked glass jewels are available in many colors, and the round shape is a pleasing contrast to traditional glass tesserae. They are especially fun to use on outdoor pieces that will be displayed in sunny spots.

4 SEA GLASS
Frosted sea glass provides a softer alternative to reflective glass tiles. Shards can be found at the beach, or purchased in bulk from a mosaic supply store.

5 BUTTONS W/PICTURES ON THEM
Many buttons offer a smooth, intricate shape that would be impossible to cut from glass or ceramic, and they can have unusual details like the ones shown here.

6 FABRIC FLOWERS
Fabric flowers are usually used to decorate garments or other sewn items, but when used in a mosaic, they add a delicate, tactile element.

7 SHAPED BUTTONS
Sewing notions suppliers often sell novelty buttons in every imaginable shape, making it easy to find something suitable for nearly any theme.

8 WOODEN GAME PIECES
Wooden pieces like these dominoes are perfect for repeating patterns.

9 PLASTER FACES, CAMEOS
Plaster is available in a multitude of shapes, both intricate and simple, and is easily painted, gilded, or stained. You can even mold your own customized shapes.

Materials

wood-backed frame

vitreous glass tiles

sea glass

clear, flat-backed glass beads

palette knife

tile nippers

soft, lint-free cloth

cement

natural gray sanded grout

acrylic admixture

grout sealant

kitchen scrubbing pad

safety goggles

work gloves

latex gloves

mixing bowls for cement
and grout

Artist: Aimee Southworth

Seascape Mirror

The vitreous glass tiles used in this mosaic shimmer beautifully in an outdoor setting.

When planning an ocean-themed design such as the one here, the boundless variety and

colors of sea life are sure to be inspiring. Refer to photographs of favorite sea creatures or

seascapes, and use them as starting points for creating a simplified mosaic version. When

selecting a frame, make sure it has a flat, wide border that will accommodate the design.

STARTING OUT   An intricate design such as this one requires planning. First, sketch out a pattern to the scale of the frame, making notes of the colors to be used in each area. Then, transfer the drawing to the frame using graphite paper. Use the lines as a guide when applying tiles.

STEP 1   Wearing safety goggles and sturdy work gloves to protect hands from sharp edges, nip an assortment of blue and green vitreous glass tiles into various shapes and sizes for the background and seaweed border of the frame. Keep the colors separated. Custom cut the colors for the images, such as the fish and sand dollars, as they are needed.

Tip: Remove the mirror before beginning the mosaic to prevent it from getting scratched.

STEP 2   Prepare the cement for outdoor use (see page 15). Using a flexible palette knife, spread a 1/8-inch (3-mm) -thick layer of cement on the back of the glass bead bubbles and place them randomly around the frame. Next, apply the tiles for each image, custom cutting tiles as they are needed. Then, use several shades of green tiles to create the undulating reed border. Randomly alternate the shades of green tiles when applying them to produce a naturalistic effect. When everything else is completed, spread cement over a 6-inch (15-cm) -square area on the frame using a palette knife, and begin applying the blue tiles to fill the background. Continue until the background is filled. Cut pieces as needed with nippers for the hard-to-fit areas around the images and the reeds. Let it dry for twenty-four hours.

Tip: The closer the tiles are to each other, the more unified a mosaic will look after grouting. This also makes the colors in a piece appear more intense.

Tip: Try incorporating items such as shells and sea glass to enhance an ocean-inspired design.

STEP 3   Prepare grout for outdoor use (see page 15), then apply a small amount on the frame with glove-protected hands. Natural gray sanded grout was used here. Work the grout completely into the crevices between the tiles using a circular motion. Continue until all the spaces between the tiles are filled. When the grout has dried enough to become powdery, no more than fifteen to twenty minutes, remove residual grout with a wet sponge. Be sure to clean the sponge often. Then, take a soft, lint-free cloth and buff the tiles. When the grout is completely dry, which will take a few days, depending on humidity, apply grout sealant according to the manufacturer's directions. Finally, replace the mirror in the frame and secure it with epoxy or weatherproof adhesive suitable for bonding glass and wood.

Tip: A thin layer of grout will finish the edges of a frame nicely. Add water to the grout mixture until the consistency is soupy, then use your hands or a paintbrush to apply it.

Materials

cement birdbath

broken ceramic tiles and dishes

china casserole cover

small rocks for borders

palette knife

hammer

tile nippers

cement

dark blue or charcoal grout, tan grout

acrylic admixture

grout sealant

kitchen scrubbing pad

safety goggles

latex gloves

filter mask

mixing bowls for cement and grout

Mixed-Tile Birdbath

**Artist: Susan
Strouse/Artful Gardens**

This piece incorporates different types of tiles and grout colors and is a fun way to expand mosaic skills. Solid and patterned ceramic shards, small rocks, and a three-dimensional ceramic focal point make a striking combination, and are challenging to fit together in a pleasing way. Begin with a pedestal or tabletop cement birdbath, found at home-and-garden centers.

Make sure it is designed for practical use. Follow the instructions for weatherproofing exactly to ensure that the bath lasts for years to come.

Several different colors of grout were used to accentuate the various ceramic pieces on this birdbath. A dark grout, such as navy blue or charcoal, blends well with the maroon shards used on the pedestal and basin. A lighter grout, such as tan, works well with the mustard and white shards seen here.

STEP 1

Wearing safety goggles and protective gloves, break the ceramics to be used into shards using a hammer (see page 20 for guidance). Medium-size pieces, about 1 to 2 inches (3 to 5 cm), will work well for most of this project. Use tile nippers to refine the size and shape of the shards as necessary. Sponge the surface of the birdbath to remove any dust or dirt.

STEP 2

Prepare the cement for outdoor use (see page 15). Starting with the base of the birdbath, use a flexible palette knife to apply a 1/8-inch (3-mm) -thick layer of cement over a 6-inch (15-cm) -square area. Press the shards into the cement one at a time, applying more cement as needed. If the base is heavily textured or uneven, apply the cement to the back of the shards instead.

Next, apply curved shards along curved areas of the basin. The white bottom ridges of mugs were used here to create the continuous line around the bath. Then, place rocks one at a time using a thicker layer of cement around the top edge of the basin. To finish the interior of the bath, first apply three reconstructed china plate images and a dimensional center piece. A casserole cover was used here. Then, fill in the rest of the space with solid colored shards. Let it dry for twenty-four hours.

VARIATION

Coordinate the colors and motifs of the mosaic with the area the birdbath will be placed in. The blue-and-green color scheme of the bath here will look beautiful nestled in a wooded space or surrounded by lush foliage. Experiment with several color themes before deciding what to use. An easy way to do this is to spread out possible tiles against a neutral background in the area where the birdbath will be installed.

STEP 3 · Prepare grout for outdoor use (see page 15), then apply a small amount on the bath with glove-protected hands. Work the grout completely into the crevices between the shards using a circular motion. Continue until all the spaces between the shards are filled. Keep wiping excess grout off the surface of the shards, because it will be difficult to sand off once dry. When the grout has dried enough to become powdery, no more than fifteen to twenty minutes, use a dry kitchen scrubbing pad to sand excess grout off the surface of the ceramic shards. Wear a filter mask while sanding. If the scrubbing pad scratches the glaze, wipe off excess grout while it is wet with a damp sponge, let it dry, then buff with a lint-free rag. When the grout is completely dry, which will take a few days, depending on humidity, apply grout sealant according to the manufacturer's directions.

Photo by Susan Strouse

Tip: Grout sealers may not be enough to prevent some china pieces from frost damage. To be on the safe side, cover the birdbath with a tarp during winter or take it inside.

Materials

rocks

broken ceramic pieces

palette knife

hammer

tile nippers

cement

grout

acrylic admixture

grout sealant

kitchen scrubbing pad

safety goggles

latex gloves

filter mask

mixing bowls for cement and grout

Ornamental Garden Rocks

These playful garden accents are the perfect showcase for ceramic

shards. Any rock can be used—egg-shaped or multifaceted rocks work espe-

Artist: Susan
Strouse/Artful Gardens and
Doreen Mastandrea

cially well. Since the pattern is free-form, odd bits and pieces can be used

without much preparation, making this a great way to use a handful of

collected shards that aren't appropriate for other projects. Choose colors

that complement the ornamental plantings in your garden.

Use brightly colored shards to create striking, monochromatic garden gems.
Choose ceramics in several shades of the same hue for maximum impact,
and select a grout color that will enhance the color scheme.

STEP 1   Wearing safety goggles and protective gloves,
break the ceramics to be used into shards using
a hammer (see page 20 for guidance). Use tile
nippers to refine the size and shape of the
shards as necessary.

STEP 2   Prepare cement for outdoor use (see page 15)
and apply a 1/8-inch (3-mm) -thick layer to a
small area of the rock. Press the shards into the
cement one at a time, applying more cement as
needed. Cover the entire rock. Let it dry for
twenty-four hours.

Tip: Always use a dry kitchen scrubbing pad when sanding
grout. A wet pad will moisten the grout, creating a film on the
shards as you sand.

VARIATION

Softer shades like the blue of these "robin's eggs" have a subtle charm. Rather than using only smooth pieces, the ridged bottoms and edges of dishes were whimsically incorporated into this design, calling attention to the previous use of the shards.

Artist: Susan Strouse/Artful Gardens

STEP 3

Prepare grout for outdoor use (see page 15), then apply it over a large area of the rock with glove-protected hands. Work the grout completely into the crevices between the shards using a circular motion. Continue until all the spaces between the shards are filled. Keep wiping excess grout off the surface of the shards, because it will be difficult to sand off once dry. When the grout has dried enough to become powdery, no more than fifteen to twenty minutes, use a dry kitchen scrubbing pad to sand excess grout off the surface of the ceramic shards. Wear a filter mask while sanding. Test the scrubbing pad on an extra shard first. If the scrubbing pad scratches the glaze, wipe off excess grout while it is wet with a damp sponge, let it dry, then buff with a lint-free rag. When the grout is completely dry, which will take a few days, depending on humidity, apply grout sealant according to the manufacturer's directions.

Tip: Any remaining sharp edges can be filed down using medium- to large-grit sandpaper or a metal file.

Materials

animal form

broken ceramic pieces in bright, solid colors

hammer

tile nippers

cement

dark gray or black grout

acrylic admixture

grout sealant

kitchen scrubbing pad

safety goggles

latex gloves

filter mask

mixing bowls for cement and grout

Garden Animals

These charming creatures are a fun way to liven up any outdoor space,

especially a garden. A search of local yard sales, thrift stores, or home-and-

garden centers is sure to yield a treasure trove of interesting and unique

outdoor sculpture. Collect the tesserae for this project from broken,

orphaned, or found ceramic dishware and tiles to give them new life.

Any one of the forms seen above is a perfect candidate for this project, because nearly every surface is suitable for mosaic work.

Artist: Doreen Mastandrea

When selecting a form, be sure it will weather well and consider how difficult it will be to cover any crevices or tight areas with tesserae.

STEP 1 | Wearing safety goggles and protective gloves, break the ceramics to be used into shards using a hammer (see page 20 for guidance). Use tile nippers to refine the size and shape of the shards as necessary. Clean and dry the animal form to be used.

STEP 2 | Prepare cement for outdoor use (see page 15), and apply a 1/8-inch (3-mm) -thick layer to a small area of the animal. Press the shards into the cement one at a time, applying more cement as needed. Cover the entire animal. Let it dry for twenty-four hours.

Tip: In tight spots, it may be easier and neater to apply the cement to the back of the tile rather than to the form.

The fluid lines of this
wire rooster are the
perfect complement to
ceramic tile work.

VARIATION

In this project, the shards are laid in a pattern reminiscent of a real bird's markings, but the colors used are whimsical rather than realistic. Consult photographs of animals to plan the placement of shards, but use your imagination when deciding on a color scheme. This combination of techniques is sure to create a striking design.

Artist: Susan Strouse/Artful Gardens

STEP 3

Prepare grout for outdoor use (see page 15), then apply it over a large area of the animal with glove-protected hands. Work the grout completely into the crevices between the shards using a circular motion. Be careful not to leave too much grout on the surface of the shards, because it will be difficult to sand off. When the grout has dried enough to become powdery, use a dry kitchen scrubbing pad to sand excess grout off the surface of the ceramic shards. Wear a filter mask while sanding. When the grout is completely dry, which will take a few days, depending on humidity, apply one coat of grout sealant.

Tip: When sanding grout, be sure to use a light-duty kitchen scrubbing pad that is safe for ceramic surfaces.

Tip: Use cups to create curved shards that fit perfectly on rounded surfaces.

Artist: Melissa Glen/Melissa Glen Mosaics
Photo by Melissa Glen

Materials

terra cotta saucer

stoneware clay

canvas

ceramic underglaze and overglaze paint in various colors

brushes

rolling pin

paring knife

tracing paper

cement

premixed white unsanded grout for outdoor use

acrylic admixture

safety goggles

latex gloves

filter mask

mixing bowls for cement and grout

Trout Rain Catcher

This mosaic is built on a terra cotta saucer, using handmade tesserae.

Stoneware clay, access to a kiln, and some simple handbuilding techniques

are all you need to start making specialized, custom tiles in any shape or

size. Many pottery studios offer a firing service for a small fee, eliminating

the need to buy a kiln or learn how to use one. Just be sure to bring in the

manufacturer's firing information for the clay and glazes used, so that the

kiln master can properly fire the pieces.

Illustrator: Mary Newell DePalma

STARTING OUT — Draw the outline of a fish on a piece of tracing paper to make a pattern. Field guides or photographic marine-life books are great sources of inspiration, both for the shape of the fish and for the color scheme. Prepare a pattern by sizing the illustration to your selected tabletop. You can enlarge the pattern in sections using a copier, or sketch or photocopy the illustration onto graph paper to determine scale.

STEP 1 — On a piece of canvas secured to a work table, use a rolling pin to flatten a piece of stoneware clay approximately 1/4 inch (7 mm) to 1/2 inch (1 cm) thick. Let that clay rest for about thirty minutes. Place the fish pattern on top of the slab of clay, then cut it out using a paring knife. Cut the remainder of the slab carefully into small squares and rectangles. These will be used to fill the area around the fish. Do not pick up or move the fish or tiles until the clay has dried enough to become rigid. At this point, they can be handled without deforming them.

Next, paint the trout using ceramic underglazes. Then, cut the fish into several tiles. The tail and fins were cut into separate tiles on this fish. Let the clay dry completely, which will take several days, then fire the fish and tiles to cone 2.

Finally, paint a clear overglaze on the once-fired trout, and paint a colored overglaze on the tiles. Apply the paint according to the manufacturer's directions. Fire all the pieces according to the manufacturer's recommendation, usually cone 06 to cone 2.

STEP 2 — Prepare the cement for outdoor use (see page 15). Using a flexible palette knife, apply an 1/8-inch (3-mm) layer of cement to the saucer. Beginning with the fish, press the tiles into the cement one at a time, applying more cement as needed. Then, fill in the background leaving the edge exposed to show off the natural terra cotta. Let it dry for twenty-four hours.

STEP 3   With glove-protected hands, apply a small amount of premixed unsanded grout for outdoor use on the rain catcher. Work the grout completely into the crevices between the tiles using a circular motion. Keep wiping excess grout off the surface of the tiles. When the grout has dried enough to become powdery, no more than fifteen to twenty minutes, use a damp sponge to clean the tiles. Rinse the sponge frequently, and wipe the tiles until all the grout film is gone. Let it dry, then buff with a rag. When the grout is completely dry, which will take a few days, depending on humidity, apply grout sealant according to the manufacturer's directions.

VARIATION

The Idea of a central custom tile can be applied to an unlimited number of themes and is the perfect way to further personalize a mosaic. Create a reusable cardboard pattern if making more than one tile, or try using specialty cookie cutters for quicker tiles.

Illustrator: Mary Newell DePalma

BITS & PIECES:
TESSERAE FROM NATURE

The inherent range of colors and patterns in natural materials such as marble, pebbles, rocks, and shells can be inspiring to work with. Marble is a classic material for floors and will lend an air of sophistication and history to a project. Stones of all kinds are perfect for outdoor pieces because they are durable and blend easily into a natural setting. Seashells come in such a gorgeous array of textures and intriguing forms that they can be used exclusively in endless ways. While all these materials are widely available for purchase, a leisurely scavenger hunt around the countryside or the seashore is the most enjoyable way to discover and collect natural tesserae.

1 MARBLE
Marble is available in a range of beautifully variegated earth tones. It can be used to make striking and unusual mosaics by combining several contrasting colors and by taking advantage of interesting streaks and patterns. It can be polished to a glasslike finish or to a more natural, matte finish. Since the shinier finish reflects more light and attracts the eye, try using both kinds within the same mosaic to call attention to specific areas.

1

2 SMALL, DARK ROCKS

A stone mosaic doesn't necessarily have to be neutral. These rocks have streaks of vibrant metallic color running through them, which will add sparkle and depth to a piece. Try combining especially beautiful or bright rocks with subtle, uniformly colored pebbles and stones so that they stand out.

3 GRAYISH, FLAT STONES

Smooth, naturally polished pebbles like these river rocks are perfectly at home in an outdoor space. Try using them to pave an area of the garden or to make stepping stones. The subtle, comforting shapes and colors of the stones here would make a serene, subtle, but inviting mosaic. The early mosaics of the ancient Greeks consisted of pebbles. For inspiration, try looking at photographs in art history books of these classic designs.

4 SHELLS

Shells of all shapes and sizes make a perfect mosaic component. Use them whole or broken, depending on the planned design. Tiny shells of the same variety can be used whole to make simple, linear patterns. Small shards created from very large shells can be used to fill a background without having to worry about matching colors. Many shells also have an iridescent sheen, especially when polished. Use these for an opulent, jeweled effect.

5 THREE LARGE ROCKS

Rocks like these were used to make the border around the birdbath on page 80. Bulky rocks add an organic dimension to a mosaic, and their natural shape is often full of character. Rocks with bands of color provide an additional design element that can be used to delineate an area, make a simple pattern, or even spell something out. Be sure to partially submerge rocks like these in a liberal amount of adhesive cement to secure them.

Materials

1/2-inch (1-cm) -thick plywood cut to desired shape

2 eye screws

picture-hanging wire

sandpaper

assorted china plates

stained glass shards

assorted found objects for accent pioeces

palette knife or craft stick

hammer

tile nippers

combination scorer and pliers

cement

grout

acrylic admixture

kitchen scrubbing pad

safety goggles

latex gloves

filter mask

mixing bowls for cement and grout

dry, lint-free cloth

Artist: Sara Curtis

House-Number Plaque

This mixed-media plaque combines glass and china tiles for a unique, fun, flea-market feel.

The numbers are made of stained-glass shards, and the borders and dimensional pieces

are ceramic. First decide on a theme or color scheme, then accumulate pieces that fit

within that framework. Seek out plates with interesting borders, images that share similar

colors, and three-dimensional pieces that relate to one another. The mushroom on the top

of this plaque is an antique salt shaker!

STARTING OUT　　Custom cut a piece of plywood for this plaque using a jigsaw, or order a piece to the desired specifications from a lumberyard. It's extremely helpful to draw or trace the entire design on the plywood before beginning to apply tiles.

STEP 1

Wearing safety goggles and protective gloves, break the ceramics to be used into shards using a hammer (see page 20 for guidance). Use tile nippers to refine the size and shape of the shards as necessary. To cut the glass pieces for the numbers, use a combination scorer and plier. First, score the section of glass to be cut, applying firm, even pressure. Then, grasp the glass with the tool and align the scoring with the guide mark. Press firmly, and the glass should snap off along the score mark. Keep the pieces organized as they are cut for easy installation by laying them out on a sketched paper pattern.

Tip: Use a stencil for the numbers or create one using computer fonts and a printer, then trace them on the board.

STEP 2

Prepare cement for outdoor use (see on page 15 for guidance). Starting with the numbers, use a palette knife or craft stick to apply a 1/8-inch (3-mm) -thick layer of cement on the wooden board. Begin applying the glass pieces, custom nipping the tiles as needed to fit them within the number stencils. Fit the glass tiles closely together. Next, fill in a solid-colored background behind the numbers so they will read clearly. Apply cement over a 6-inch (15-cm) -square area at a time. Be sure the adhesive doesn't squeeze into the crevices between the tiles. Next, begin applying the border pieces along the edges of the plaque and add any additional elements. Let it dry for twenty-four hours.

Tip: If a design calls for a lot of intricate cutting around images or three-dimensional pieces, look into renting a wet saw from a home center for the day. It will make the process quicker and easier. Carefully follow the manufacturer's instructions for use.

STEP 3

Prepare grout for outdoor use (see page 15), then apply a small amount to the plaque with glove-protected hands. Work the grout completely into the crevices between the tiles using a circular motion. Continue until all the spaces between the tiles are filled. Keep wiping excess grout off the surface of the tiles. Once grouting is completed, use a damp sponge to wipe off any excess. Let it dry, then buff with a lint-free rag. Finally, apply hardware such as eye screws and picture-hanging wire for installation.

Tip: Let the border pieces extend off of the plaque. This is an easy and effective way to conceal the unfinished edges.

Materials

metal mailbox

flat-backed glass beads in
various colors

palette knife or craft stick

cement

acrylic admixture

black sanded grout

grout sealant

kitchen scrubbing pad

latex gloves

filter mask

mixing bowls for cement and
grout

Artist: Robin Millman

Tool Mailbox

A plain, purely utilitarian metal mailbox from a home center was covered with flat-backed

glass beads to make this outdoor toolbox – a beautiful solution for keeping tools organized

and protected from the elements after a busy day of gardening. It can also be used as a fun,

funky alternative to a traditional mailbox. Black grout was used to make these ordinary

glass beads pop out, transforming them into glistening gems as they catch sunlight.

STARTING OUT
Flat-backed glass beads in various colors and sizes can be purchased from stained-glass or craft supply stores. Use contrasting classic colors such as the red, green, yellow, and blue seen here for a dramatic, vibrant effect. Be sure to rough up the surface of the metal to ensure good adhesion.

STEP 1
Prepare cement for outdoor use (see page 15 for guidance). Lay the mailbox on one side. Starting on the bottom edge, use a craft stick or flexible palette knife to spread a 1/8-inch (3-mm) -thick layer of mortar over a small area. Begin applying the beads closely together. Green and yellow were used here to create a border pattern. Continue until the edge is complete. Let the mortar set up for ten to fifteen minutes. Then, stand the mailbox upright and begin applying beads to cover the top and sides. Let the finished side dry completely, then lay the mailbox on that side and cover the other bottom edge with beads. Next, apply beads to the front and back ends of the mailbox. Finally, apply accent beads to the front latch and the flag. Blue, green, red, and yellow beads were used here. Let it dry for twenty-four hours.

Tip: It can be difficult to secure beads to a plastic flag. If possible, use a mailbox with a metal flag.

Tip: Make sure the consistency of the mortar is thick enough to hold the beads in place securely, so that they won't slide on the mailbox's curved surface.

STEP 2
Prepare grout for outdoor use (see page 15), then apply a small amount on the mailbox with glove-protected hands. Work the grout completely into the crevices between the beads using a circular motion. Continue until all the spaces between the beads are filled. Keep wiping excess grout off the surface of the beads, so that the glass can be easily cleaned once the grout is dry.

STEP 3
When the grout has dried enough to become powdery, no more than fifteen to twenty minutes, use a dry kitchen scrubbing pad to sand excess grout off the surface of the beads. Wear a filter mask while sanding. Try to uncover as much of the beads as possible. Then, use a soft, dry cloth to buff the beads. When the grout is completely dry, which will take a few days, depending on humidity, apply grout sealant according to the manufacturer's directions.

Materials

birdhouse form

broken china pieces

palette knife

hammer

tile nippers

cement

white sanded grout

acrylic admixture

grout sealant

kitchen scrubbing pad

safety goggles

latex gloves

filter mask

mixing bowls for cement and grout

Artist: Doreen Mastandrea

China Birdhouse

China dishware provides an unlimited resource for patterns that can be used in mosaic work. Before adhering the shards, play with the placement possibilities of the design elements on the plates and cups. A running vine or repeating floral pattern can be put back together or rearranged in a new way. Here, a cup handle was used for the bird perch, and a gold-rimmed saucer was used to delineate the edge of the roof.

STARTING OUT   Choose cups and plates that share many of the same colors, but have different patterns. This helps to unify the piece when using mismatched china. The colors used here are predominantly red, pink, pale yellow, various leaf greens, and white.

STEP 1   Wearing safety goggles and protective gloves, break the china plates and cups to be used into shards using a hammer (see page 20 for guidance). Use tile nippers to refine the size and shape of the shards as necessary.

Tip: Keep the tile nippers handy to custom cut pieces for hard-to-fit areas, and to cut out flowers or other interesting patterns from the plates.

STEP 2   Prepare the cement for outdoor use (see page 15). Using a flexible palette knife, apply a 1/8 -inch (3-mm) -thick layer of cement over a small area on one side of the birdhouse. Press the shards into the cement one at a time, applying more cement as needed. Be careful to keep the cement off the top of the china. It will be difficult to clean off once the mixture dries. Continue until all the sides are covered. Let it dry for twenty-four hours.

STEP 3   Prepare grout for outdoor use (see page 15), then apply a small amount over one side of the birdhouse with glove-protected hands. Work the grout completely into the crevices between the shards using a circular motion. Continue until all the spaces between the shards are filled. Keep wiping excess grout off the surface of the china because it will be difficult to sand off once dry. Be careful in delicate places such as the perch and roofline. When the grout has dried enough to become powdery, no more than fifteen to twenty minutes, use a dry kitchen scrubbing pad to sand excess grout off the surface of the ceramic shards. Wear a filter mask while sanding. Test the scrubbing pad on an extra shard first. If the scrubbing pad scratches the glaze, wipe off excess grout while it is wet with a damp sponge, let it dry, then buff with a lint-free rag. When the grout is completely dry, which will take a few days, depending on humidity, apply grout sealant according to the manufacturer's directions.

Tip: Always use a dry kitchen scrubbing pad to sand excess grout, because moisture and grout dust create a film on china that is difficult to clean.

BITS & PIECES:
PIQUE ASSIETTE

Pique assiette, a French term that literally means stolen from plate, is a mosaic style that transforms into works of art broken or orphaned ceramic pieces such as china plates, teacups, figurines, and other odds and ends that are otherwise destined for the trash. Part of the fun of this addictive, recycling-oriented form of mosaic is cruising flea markets, antique stores, yard sales, and even the attic, looking for unique ceramics. For an especially personal "memoryware" mosaic, try using those chipped or damaged family heirlooms that you just can't part with to create something new.

Some ceramics can be damaged by frost, so take this into consideration before planning an outdoor project. Always weatherproof a china mosaic, and to be on the safe side, bring the piece indoors or cover it with a tarp during winter.

1 **CUPS WITH GOLD AND BLUE EDGE**
China often features beautiful metallic glazes that can be used to great effect. The edges of these cups could be reassembled to make a glittering border for a mosaic image.

2 **STACKED PLATES UNDER BIRD**
The variety of glaze colors is endless, and the same glaze can change slightly from piece to piece even in a matched set. Try using only two colors to create a harmonious, understated design. One traditional and popular pairing in ceramics is blue and white. Incorporating a range of shades in a single hue will lend interest and elegance to a piece.

3 PILE OF PLATES WITH A HEART-SHAPED BOX ON TOP

In addition to dishware, look for other ceramic items such as vases, planters, lamp bases, or boxes like the heart-shaped one here. Small to medium-sized box covers can be used almost like tiles and need very little, if any, preparation.

4 CUP AND SAUCER SET WITH NAVY-BLUE EDGES

China is often covered with gorgeous patterns that can be creatively reassembled for a mosaic (see the birdhouse project on page 104 for tips on how to do this). Elements of a pattern, such as the flowers on this cup, are easy to trim out of delicate china using tile nippers. Take advantage of small-scale elegant floral designs to create a set of traditionally sized tiles.

5 UPSIDE-DOWN TEACUP

An ornate teacup handle, such as the one here, was used to make the perch for the birdhouse on page 104. Take advantage of the open, delicate shape to create vinelike patterns.

6 PLATE WITH WIDE, WAVY YELLOW EDGE

Plates can be used to make easy, continuous borders. The solid-colored, wavy edge of this one is simple but elegant – the perfect complement to a complex or ornately patterned design.

3

5

4

6

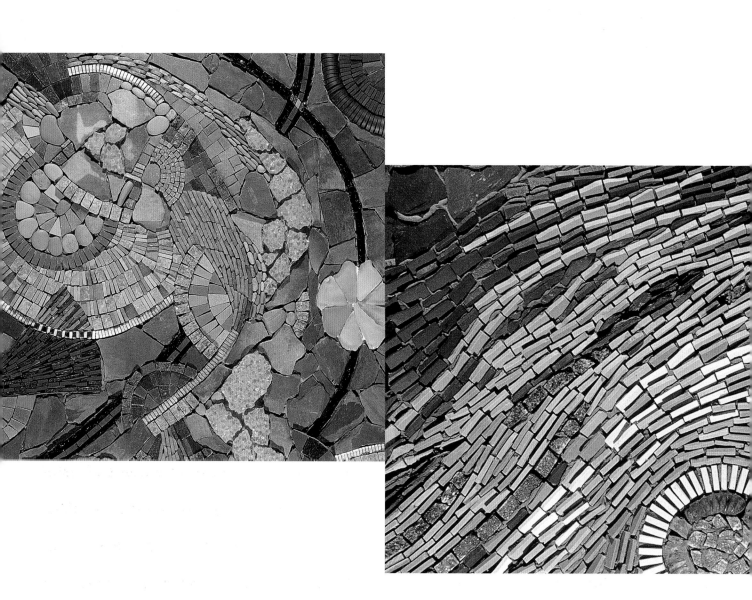

Gallery

The projects in this book can be completed by any beginner, and they provide all the know-how and practice you need to progress to the next step: the making of more challenging, personal, and expressive mosaics. The installations pictured in the Gallery were created by professional mosaic artists, and we include them in hopes that they will encourage your creativity. Use them as a starting point for designing your own original works.

The different style of each Gallery artist suggests new and distinctive ways to approach your personal mosaic efforts. Since you can use a multitude of materials to make a mosaic, and there are endless ways to arrange the tiles, designing a project from scratch can be overwhelming. A sure way to get focused is to look at beautiful, professional pieces and analyze how they are put together.

Finally, don't be intimidated by professional pieces – everyone starts somewhere. Desire and a little practice are all you need to make a good mosaic. Let the works of these fellow mosaic artists serve as both inspiration and motivation, and may the muses be with you.

Porcelain tile; 10 feet (305 cm) by 4 feet (122 cm).

Title: Quilts

Artists: Twin Dolphin Mosaics, Stephanie Jurs and Robert Stout

These floor panels were inspired by quilts. Quilt patterns lend themselves to mosaic work because of their graphic shapes and focus on color. Look to other traditional artwork, such as stained glass, for more ideas and motifs.

Broken ceramic tile; 8 feet (244 cm) by 4 feet (122 cm).

Title: Children's Clinic Mosaic

Artists: Twin Dolphin Mosaics, Stephanie Jurs and Robert Stout

Many mosaic artists are commissioned to do murals; this piece was commissioned by a children's health clinic. A successful mural starts with planning and a good design. The fanciful, childlike imagery here is both comforting and cheerful – just the thing to brighten a health care facility. By tailoring your design to suit the place where it will be installed, you make sure that the piece will be seamlessly integrated into its surroundings.

**Broken ceramic tile; eight 4-foot (122-cm)
by 4-foot (122-cm) panels.**

Title: Pear Wall Hanging

Artists: Twin Dolphin Mosaics, Stephanie Jurs and Robert Stout

This simple image of a pear illustrates how any image can be trans-
lated into individual dots of color. Seen from a distance, the colors
blend into one smooth image. A computer can help easily translate a
photo into a mosaic template – just enlarge the image until each
pixel, or dot, is evident. Historically, fruits appear in many mosaics.
Look through books on historical mosaics for more inspiration.

aBroken ceramic tile; eight 4-foot (122-cm) by 4-foot (122-cm) panels.

Title: Tile Floor Installation

Artist: Andrew Martin

This floor installation demonstrates how anything can be depicted in a mosaic. The scale of this architectural piece makes a huge impact, drawing the viewer into the work. The grout lines are spaced evenly to give the piece a clean look. An image of pizza or other foods would work well on the floor of a large kitchen.

Glass smalti and gold.

Title: Tropical Bouquet II

Artist: George Fishman

This piece combines glass smalti and opulent gold tiles for a classic, traditional look. The materials used in a project are as important as the design, so consider the desired effect before selecting tiles. Imagine this mosaic made with ceramic shards; the overall piece would be looser and more casual.

Broken ceramic tile; eight 4-foot (122-cm) by 4-foot (122-cm) panels.

Title: Byzantine Fantasy I

Artist: George Fishman

Since every picture can be broken into individual bits of color, mosaics are the perfect medium for illustrating scenes like this one. Reminiscent of an ancient tapestry, this mosaic shows how individual tiles can coalesce into one remarkably detailed image.

Slate, glass, marble, stone, aluminum, mirror, ceramic, and other materials; 27 3/4 inches (70 cm) by 20 1/2 inches (52 cm).

Title: Hill Country

Artist: Sonia King

This piece, crafted entirely of natural materials, transforms a simple linear pattern into a wonderfully detailed landscape. It's not necessary to begin with an intricate pattern to make a successful mosaic. Paying attention to each tile's color and texture adds depth to a piece like this one, making it easier to convey a complex design idea with a simple pattern.

Slate, ceramic tile, marble, and fossils; 20 inches (51 cm) by 14 1/4 inches (36 cm).

Title: Riverscape

Artist: Sonia King

This work uses only a few simple shapes to successfully depict a river scene. The key to getting a design idea across in a mosaic is to identify the elements that will make it recognizable. Simplify an image, such as a photo, as much as possible, and try to figure out which lines and shapes are crucial.

Broken ceramic tile, china, and glass.

Title: Patio Table

Photo: Picture Press: Schöner Wohnen

This patio table is a perfect example of how to use your favorite plates or family heirlooms to create a dynamic new piece of mosaic furniture. Each place setting includes a fork, knife, and coffee cup adding whimsy to a sophisticated design.

Slate, marble, and granite; 8 inches (20 cm) by 26 inches (66 cm).

Title: Rio de la Roca

Artist: Sonia King

Mosaic design can be representative or abstract. This triptych shows the "movement" of a river through the placement and size of the stones. Playing with these elements you can create different types of effects. Using color to "shape" the formal elements also works in an interesting way to create movement.

Vitreous glass, limestone, ceramic, and shell; 16 inches (41 cm) by 23 inches (58 cm).

Title: Moon River

Artist: Sonia King

The narrow tiles used here to make undulating patterns suggest the currents and eddies of a river. Paired with subtle variations in color, these tiles accurately convey the feeling of gentle running water. When putting together a mosaic, try to use tiles with shapes that suggest certain emotions or sensations.

Marble, glass, ceramic, shell, soapstone, granite, and other materials; 18 1/2 inches (47 cm) by 26 inches (66 cm).

Title: Primeval

Sonia King

The combination of glazed ceramic tiles and pebbles in this piece creates an interesting interplay between shiny and matte surfaces. By using pieces with different surface textures, the artist keeps the viewer interested in all elements of the design.

Resources

Glass Crafters Stained Glass Inc.
398 Interstate Court
Sarasota, FL 34240
800-422-4552
http://glasscrafters.com

Mosaic Matters
The online magazine for all things mosaic
www.users.dircon.co.uk/~asm/index.htm

Mosaic Mercantile
P.O. Box 78206
San Francisco, CA 94107
877-966-7242
http://mosaicmercantile.com

Mountaintop Mosaics
Elm Street
P.O. Box 653
Castleton, VT 05735
800-564-4980
www.mountaintopmosaics.com

Mosaic Workshop
1a Princeton Street
London, England
WC1R 4AX
02-7831-0889
www.mosaicworkshop.com

National Artcraft Co.
7996 Darrow Road
Twinsburg, OH 44087
888-937-2723

The Partner One Corporation
(wrought iron tables)
458 Satinwood Way
Chula Vista, CA 91911
800-474-7168

TileMosaics.com
P.O. Box 15101
Long Beach, CA 90815
562-715-6511
www.tilemosaics.com

Wits End Mosaics
5224 West State Road 46
Box 134
Sanford, FL 32771
407-323-9122

Contributors

Twyla Arthur
2007 West Summit
San Antonio, TX 78201
twylaa@earthlink.net

Linda Benswanger/Mozayiks
612 East 9th Street, #3
New York, NY 10009
212-677-7834

Sara Curtis
St. Louis, MO
Givethemroots@aol.com

Melissa Glen Mosaics
73 Locust Street
Holliston, MA 01746

Deb Mandile
Plum Island, MA
Dcbar1234@aol.com

Doreen Mastandrea
144 Moody Street
Waltham, MA 02453
paintaplate@juno.com

Robin Millman
Lexington, MA
daffodillish@aol.com

Aimee Southworth
Lexington, MA
southctm@aol.com

Susan Strouse/Artful Gardens
Boston, MA

Bruce Winn
Roseberry-Winn Pottery and Tile
669 Elmwood Avenue
Providence, RI 02907
www.roseberrywinn.com

Gallery Artists

Twin Dolphin Mosaics
Robert Stout and Stephanie Jurs
Via Bartolini, 8
48100 Ravenna
Italy
phone: 011-39-0544-456-345
email: sjurs@racine.ravenna.it

Robert Stout and Stephanie Jurs, an American husband-and-wife team, have been designing and creating mosaics since 1990 as Twin Dolphin Mosaics. Together they have completed numerous public art projects in the southwestern United States, ranging from large architectural pavings to small interior wall pieces. In 1998 they moved to Ravenna, Italy, an internationally renowned center of Byzantine mosaics, to study traditional Roman and Byzantine techniques.

George Fishman
103 N.E. 99 Street
Miami Shores, FL 33138
phone: 305-758-1141
email: mosaics@telocity.com
website:
www.georgefishmanmosaics.com

George Fishman became hooked on mosaics while exploring the remains of beautifully patterned fourth-century Roman floors in southwestern France. He now specializes in mosaic artwork for architectural surfaces and works with architects, interior designers, and other contractors to create installations primarily in southern Florida.

Sonia King
1023 Sarasota Circle
Dallas, TX 75223
phone: 214-824-5854
email: sonia@mosaicworks.com
website: www.mosaicworks.com

Sonia King's work is represented in private and corporate collections and exhibited both nationally and internationally. She is a founder and advisory board member of the Society of American Mosaic Artists as well as an instructor in mosaic at the Creative Arts Center of Dallas. She is the author of *The World Book of Mosaics* (Sterling Publishers).

Andrew Martin
369 B Third Street
PMB 105
San Rafael, CA 94901
email: Andrew_Martin@adidam.org

Index

About the Authors

Ceramic artist and color maven Doreen Mastandrea works in Lexington, Massachusetts, where she runs Paint a Plate Studio. Her ceramic sculptures have been shown in various galleries. She has also created numerous mosaic installations and taught mosaic workshops at several schools in the Boston area. She is the author of *Ceramic Painting Color Workshop* (Rockport Publishers).

Livia McRee is a craft author and designer who has written and contributed to many books, including *Quick Crafts* (Rockport Publishers), *Ceramic Painting Color Workshop* (Rockport Publishers), *Paper Shade* (Rockport Publishers), and *Instant Fabric: Quilted Projects from Your Home Computer* (Martingale & Company).